Letterland

My First Dictionary

Compiled by Lisa Holt

Based on characters originated by Lyn Wendon

Published 2013 by Letterland International Ltd,
Leatherhead, Surrey, KT22 9AD, UK
© Letterland International 2013
10 9 8 7 6 5 4 3 2 1

ISBN: 978-1-86209-938-8
Product Code: TE57

LETTERLAND® is a registered
trademark of Lyn Wendon.

Printed in Singapore

British Library Cataloguing in Publication Data
A catalogue record for this book is available from the British Library.

Written and compiled by: Lisa Holt
Designed by: Verity Clark
Originator of Letterland: Lyn Wendon

Contents

About this book

This book helps children acquire basic dictionary skills in a friendly and enjoyable way. The dictionary can be used to learn about the alphabet and alphabetical order, as well as how to locate words, check spellings, find simple definitions and use words in the context of a simple phrase or sentence.

The unique feature of this first dictionary is the way the Letterland characters and stories guide your child. The **a-z** characters are shown at the top of each page.

By just starting to pronounce a character's name, such as '**a**...' (Annie Apple) or '**sss**...' (Sammy Snake) a child automatically says the correct letter sound for the words on that page.

Stars indicate decodable words. These contain the letters in their most phonically regular form, making them an ideal focus for beginner readers.

① **alphabet**

② **uppercase letter**

③ **lowercase letter**

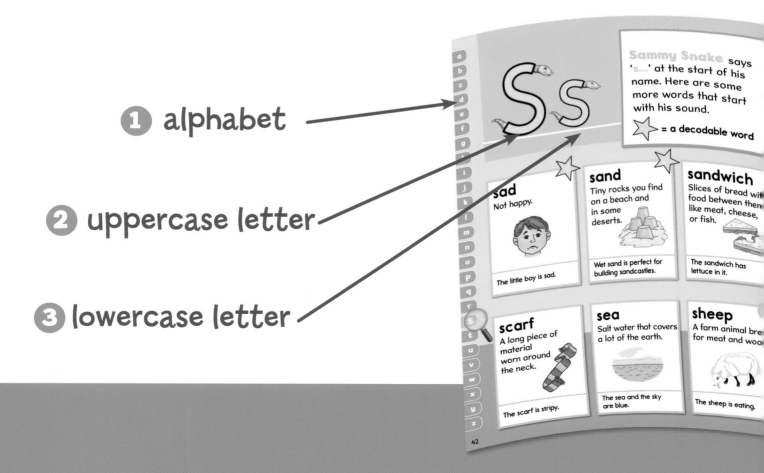

Once children have mastered the **a-z** sounds, Letterland goes on to teach how new sounds are made when letters come together in words. The stories build on what the children already know, so learning quite complex spelling rules feels more like listening to stories about friends!

Letterland has stories to teach all 44 letter sounds in the English language. This dictionary introduces just a few summaries of spelling stories to help with the first stages of reading and spelling.

The dictionary also includes more than 300 carefully chosen words, including the 100 most frequently used words in the English language.

For more information and to see our full product range please visit:
www.letterland.com

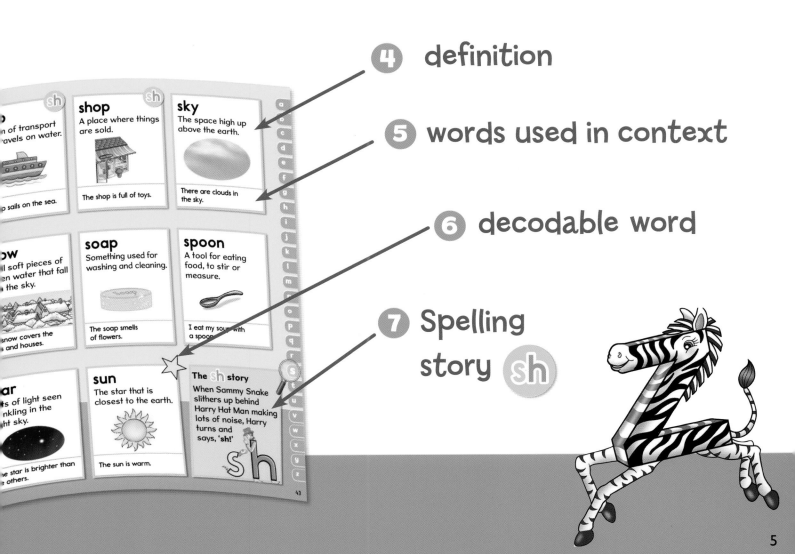

4 definition

5 words used in context

6 decodable word

7 Spelling story sh

Annie Apple says 'a...' at the start of her name. Here are some more words that start with her sound.

 = a decodable word

accident
Something that happens that isn't planned.

The paint was spilled by accident.

acrobat
Someone who can do gymnastics, often up in the air.

The acrobat swung upside down at the circus.

age
How old something is.

What age is Noisy Nick?

alien
A living being from another planet.

This alien is quite little and has big eyes.

alphabet
The letters we use when we are reading and writing.

There is an alphabet poster on the wall.

ambulance
The transport you go to hospital in if you are injured or ill.

The ambulance can go very fast.

animal

A living thing. Not a plant or a person.

This animal eats grass.

ankle

The part of the body that joins your leg and foot.

My ankle is hurting.

ant

An insect that lives in a large group or colony.

Ants have six legs.

apple

A round red, green or yellow fruit.

This apple is green and crunchy.

apron

Clothing you wear to protect the clothes underneath.

Mr A wears a red and white striped apron.

arrow

A line with a pointed end, used to point to something.

Follow the arrows to the EXIT.

astronaut

Someone who goes into space.

The astronaut is signing the book.

atlas

A book of maps.

America is in the atlas.

Mr A

This is Mr A, the Apron Man. He waves and says his name in words.

 Bouncy Ben says 'b...' at the start of his name. Here are some more words that start with his sound.

 = a decodable word

ball
A round, bouncy toy you can throw, catch or kick.

Bouncy Ben can balance a ball on his head.

balloon
A thin, stretchy, rubber toy you fill with air.

There were lots of balloons at the party.

banana
A long, curved, yellow fruit.

Bouncy Ben eats bananas for breakfast.

bath
A large tub of water you sit in to wash.

The bath is full of warm water and bubbles.

bear
A big, furry animal with a short tail.

The bear growled and ran into the woods.

bike
A form of transport with two wheels and pedals.

This bike is red.

bird

An animal with feathered wings and a beak. It lays eggs.

This is a brown bird.

boat

A form of transport that floats on water.

The boat bobbed about on the water.

book

A collection of words on lots of pages.

I like to read a book before bedtime.

box

A container made of stiff material that usually has four sides, a bottom and a lid.

The ball is by the box.

boy

A male child.

The boy is called Bob.

bread

A food made with flour and baked in an oven.

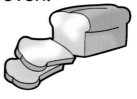

We like bread and butter for breakfast.

bridge

A structure you use to go over a river or road.

The water flows under the bridge.

brush

A tool used to tidy your hair.

The brush belongs to me.

bus

A form of transport that carries lots of people on the roads.

We will get on this bus to go to school.

Clever Cat says 'c...' at the start of her name. Here are some more words that start with her sound.

 = a decodable word

cake
A sweet food you often eat on your birthday.

Clever Cat likes to eat cake.

camera
An object for taking photos.

Look at the camera and say, 'cheese'!

car
A form of transport that has an engine and four wheels.

Clever Cat's car is red and yellow.

castle
A large, strong building built a very long time ago.

The castle is built on a hill.

chair
A piece of furniture for one person to sit on.

This chair is made from wood.

cheese
A solid food made from milk.

Cheese on toast is a tasty snack.

chicken

A farm animal raised for food.

The chicken is with its baby.

chocolate
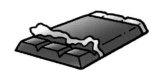
A sweet treat made from cocoa beans.

This chocolate is delicious!

clock

An object that shows the time.

The clock ticked.

cloud
It is white or grey, floats in the sky and is made up of tiny water droplets.

The clouds are white and fluffy.

cold
The opposite of hot.

The snow is cold.

computer
It stores information and helps us work and play.

My mum uses a computer at work.

cow
A female farm animal that eats grass and produces milk.
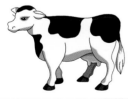

This cow is black and white.

cup
A container you drink from.

The cup is empty.

The ch story

When Clever Cat sits next to Harry Hat Man his hairy hat makes her sneeze, 'ch!'

Dippy Duck says 'd...' at the start of her name. Here are some more words that start with her sound.

 = a decodable word

dad

A man who is a parent in a family.

Dippy Duck loves her dad.

dentist

Someone who looks after your teeth.

The dentist works in a surgery.

dinosaur

An animal that lived a long time ago.

The dinosaur bones are at the museum.

doctor

Someone who looks after you if you are injured or unwell.

The doctor works at the hospital.

dog

A furry animal with four legs, that is often a pet.

The dog is running.

doll

A toy person.

The doll has long, soft hair.

door

You open it to get into a room.

The door is closed.

dress

Clothing that covers you from your shoulders to your legs.

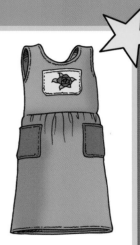

The dress is pink.

drink

A liquid you swallow.

On a hot day I like a cold drink.

drum

A musical instrument you bang with a stick or hands.

Drums make a loud noise!

duck

A bird with webbed feet that often lives near water.

The duck waddled to the duckpond.

a b c d e f g h i j k l m n o p q r s t u v w x y z

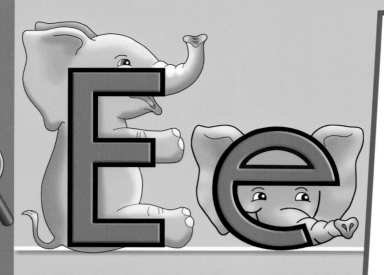

Eddy Elephant says 'e...' at the start of his name. Here are some more words that start with his sound.

 = a decodable word

eagle
A bird of prey.

The eagle sat on the rock.

ear
A part of the body used for hearing.

The boy's ears needed to be cleaned.

east
The opposite of west.

The sun rises in the east.

eat
How you take food into your body.

A monkey eats bananas.

edge
The part where two sides meet.

The pen is at the edge of the table.

egg
The shell in which a baby animal or bird can grow.

The bird laid its egg in the nest.

elbow

The part of the body that joins the upper arm to the lower arm.

It hurts if I hit my elbow.

elephant

A large grey or brown animal with a long trunk.

Elephants have two long tusks.

empty

When a container has nothing inside.

The glass is empty.

end

The last part, or when something has stopped.

That is the end of Eddy's trunk.

entrance

A place you go through to get inside.

The entrance has a big red door.

envelope

Folded paper that can hold a letter or card.

Eddy Elephant
11 Elm End
Letterland

The envelope has a stamp on it.

exercise

Doing things that improve your body or mind.

Eddy Elephant enjoys exercise.

exit

A place you go through to get outside.

The exit is through that door.

Mr E

This is Mr E, the Easy Magic Man. He waves and says his name in words.

a b c d e f g h i j k l m n o p q r s t u v w x y z

15

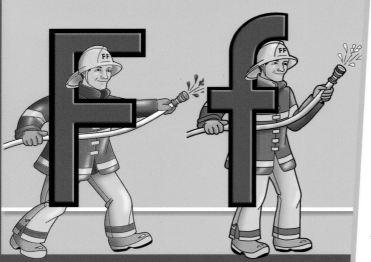

Firefighter Fred says 'f...' at the start of his name. Here are some more words that start with his sound.

 = a decodable word

fairy

An imaginary creature with special magical powers.

I think this fairy lives in a forest.

farm

A place where you grow crops or keep animals, or both.

There is a barn full of hay at this farm.

finger

A part of the body on your hands.

Can you wiggle your fingers?

fire

The light and heat when something is burning.

The fire crackled.

fish

A scaly animal that swims and lives in the water.

To swim a fish wiggles its fins.

flag

A piece of cloth that shows a symbol or colours.

The flag fluttered in the wind.

flower

The colourful part of a plant that makes fruit, seeds or vegetables.

This flower is yellow.

food

Something you can eat.

The food for lunch was fabulous.

foot

The part of the body at the end of the leg that you stand on.

The foot is on the floor.

forest

A large group of trees.

The forest is on the hill, by the sea.

fork

A tool for eating food.

I have a special fork for eating my dinner.

fox

A wild animal with a bushy tail and pointed nose.

This fox can run fast.

fridge

A place where you can keep food cold and fresh.

The fridge is full of food.

frog

A small, jumping animal that croaks.

The frog ate a fly.

fruit

The part of the plant with seeds. You can often eat it.

The fruit basket is full.

Golden Girl says 'g...' at the start of her name. Here are some more words that start with her sound.

garden

Land to enjoy, often near a house. It can have grass or plants.

Golden Girl has a lovely, green garden.

gate

Part of a wall or fence that swings to open and close.

The gate is closed.

girl

A female child.

The girl has long, golden hair.

glass

A container that holds drinks.

The glass has a straw in it.

gloves

Clothing that is worn on the hands.

My gloves got wet in the snow.

glue

A thick, sticky paste used to join things together.

The glue is in the blue pot.

goat

An animal with thick fur and horns. Some people drink its milk.

The goat went through the gate.

grapes

A small fruit with purple, red or green skin.

These grapes are green.

grass

A green plant that covers fields and gardens.

The girl is lying on the grass.

guitar

A musical instrument with strings.

The guitar makes a great sound.

a b c d e f g h i j k l m n o p q r s t u v w x y z

Harry Hat Man says 'h...' at the start of his name. Here are some more words that start with his sound.

= a decodable word

hair

It grows on your body, especially on your head.

She dries her hair with a hairdryer.

hammer

A tool with a heavy metal head, mostly used for hitting nails.

Nick hits nails with his hammer.

hand

The part of the body at the end of the arm that has fingers.

Can you wave your hand?

hat

A piece of clothing that covers your head.

Harry Hat Man wears a hairy hat.

head

The part of the body that contains the brain.

The girl has brown hair on her head.

helicopter

A form of air transport, with spinning blades on top.

The helicopter hovered up high.

20

hill

An area of high land. Smaller than a mountain.

The view from the top of the hill was good.

hippo

A large, grey animal with a big mouth and short legs.

The hippo yawned.

hole

A hollow place in something.

The mouse lives in the little hole.

holiday

A time when you do not have to go to school or work.

The holiday was hot and sunny.

honey

A thick, sweet liquid made by bees.

Honey tastes lovely on toast.

horse

A large animal that can be ridden.

Harry Hat Man made a hat for his horse!

hospital

A place where sick or injured people can get help.

The doctors and nurses work at the hospital.

hot

The opposite of cold. Very hot things can burn.

The woman felt hot in the sun.

house

A building where people can live.

The house has three windows and a red door.

a b c d e f g h i j k l m n o p q r s t u v w x y z

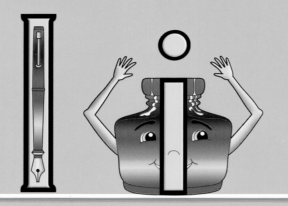

Impy Ink says 'i...' at the start of his name. Here are some more words that start with his sound.

 = a decodable word

ice
Frozen water.

Mr I likes ice in his drinks.

ice cream
A food made from frozen cream and sugar.

Ice cream melts in the sun.

idea
A thought or suggestion.

It was a good idea to make the cupcake.

ill
When someone is not well.

Impy Ink feels ill.

in
A word used to show the position or location of something.

The insect is in the box.

information
Facts that explain things.

Letterland Times

The newspaper is full of useful information.

injection

A way doctors sometimes give medicine.

The injection did not hurt at all.

ink

A coloured liquid found in pens.

The ink in this bottle is blue.

insect

A small animal with six legs, sometimes called a bug.

The buzzing sound is coming from that insect.

instrument

An object you can make music with.

The instrument is made of brass.

invitation

A request from someone asking you to go somewhere.

The invitation is to a birthday party.

iron

A tool used to make clothes smooth.

The iron is very hot.

island

A piece of land surrounded by water.

The island is sandy and hot.

itch

A feeling on the skin that makes you want to scratch.

The flea made the dog itch.

Mr I

This is Mr I, the Ice Cream Man. He waves and says his name in words.

Jumping Jim says 'j...' at the start of his name. Here are some more words that start with his sound.

= a decodable word

jacket

A short coat, usually with sleeves and a fastening at the front.

Jim's jacket is red and yellow.

jam

A sticky mixture to eat, made with fruit and sugar.

Jumping Jim likes strawberry jam.

jeans

Trousers made from a heavy material, often blue.

The girl wears jeans every day.

jeep

A type of car that can travel off the road.

The jeep went on a bumpy road.

jelly

A soft, wobbly food made from gelatine, sugar and water.

The jelly was perfect for the party.

jet

A form of air transport. It has wings and is very fast.

The jet zoomed over us.

jewel

Special stones that are bright and shiny.

The ring has a jewel on top.

jigsaw

A picture puzzle, in pieces, to put together for fun.

The jigsaw is of a jumbo jet.

juice

A liquid you can drink.

A glass of orange juice is nice at breakfast time.

jungle

Land with lots of trees, bushes and tropical plants growing in it.

The jungle is noisy at sunrise.

Kk

Kicking King says 'k...' at the start of his name. Here are some more words that start with his sound.

kangaroo

An animal with big back legs and a long tail.

The kangaroo comes from Australia.

karate

A method of using your body to protect yourself.

The karate lesson was cancelled.

kettle

A pot with a spout used for boiling water.

Be careful. A kettle can be very hot!

key

An object you use to open and close locks.

The key opens the door to the castle.

kind

Gentle and caring.

The king is kind to his kitten.

king

A man who rules a country.

This is Kicking King.

kitchen

A room where you cook food.

The cooker is in the kitchen.

kite

A toy you fly in the air at the end of a long string.

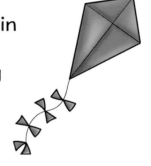

The kite's tail helps it to fly.

kitten

A young cat.

A kitten likes to play and sleep.

koala

An animal that lives in trees in Australia.

The koala is climbing the tree.

a
b
c
d
e
f
g
h
i
j
k
l
m
n
o
p
q
r
s
t
u
v
w
x
y
z

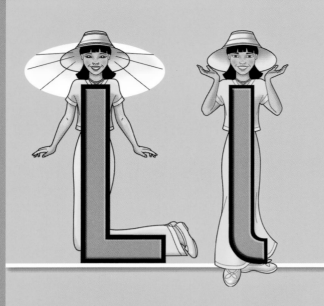

Lucy Lamp Light

says 'l...' at the start of her name. Here are some more words that start with her sound.

 = a decodable word

ladder

An object you can climb up to reach a higher place.

Lucy Lamp Light's ladder is long.

lady

A woman or a girl.

This lady likes laughing!

lake

An area of water surrounded by land.

There is snow around the lake.

lamb

A young sheep.

This little lamb has lost its mummy.

leaf

The flattest part of a plant or tree that is usually green.

Each leaf fell off the tree.

left

The opposite of right.

The lorry turned left at the traffic lights.

a b c d e f g h i j k l m n o p q r s t u v w x y z

leg

The part of the body between the hip and the ankle.

Lucy is bending her leg.

lemon

A small, yellow fruit that tastes sour.

This lemon has been picked off a tree.

leopard

A large cat with black spots.

The leopard is lying in the tree.

letter

A symbol that represents a sound in written language.

These letters spell out the word 'log'.

library

A place where you can go to borrow books.

I like going to the library with my dad.

light

The opposite of dark. It allows us to see.

The light shines brightly.

lightning

A bright flash of light in the sky.

The lightning lit up the sky.

lion

A large, strong cat with light fur.

This lion is lying down.

log

A thick piece of wood, cut from a tree.

This log was part of a big tree.

Mm

Munching Mike says 'm...' at the start of his name. Here are some more words that start with his sound.

 = a decodable word

man
A male adult.

The man is waving at me.

map
A picture of the earth as seen from above.

The map shows the way to the mountains.

mask
Something fun to wear on your face.

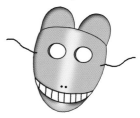

The costume includes a mask.

meat
Food from animals, such as beef, chicken or pork.

The meat is ready to eat.

melon
A fruit that is round and juicy.

The melon is juicy and refreshing.

milk
A white liquid you can drink.

The milk is in a glass.

money

Coins or paper you can use for buying things.

My grandma gives me money for my birthday.

monkey

An animal with a long tail that can swing in the trees.

The monkey likes to eat bananas.

moon

A bright object in space that goes around a planet.

The moon shines brightly in the sky.

mountain

A very big hill.

The mountain has snow on top of it.

mouse

A small animal with a long tail. It squeaks.

This mouse is scared of cats.

mud

Wet, sticky brown earth.

The mouse is covered in mud.

museum

A place where you can go to see interesting objects or art.

Let's go to the museum.

mushroom

A kind of fungus. You can eat some mushrooms.

The mushroom tastes delicious.

music

Nice sounds made by singing or playing an instrument.

Let's dance to the music.

a b c d e f g h i j k l m n o p q r s t u v w x y z

Nn

Noisy Nick says 'n...' at the start of his name. Here are some more words that start with his sound.

⭐ = a decodable word

name

The word by which something or someone is known.

The girl's name is Nat.

neck

The part of the body that connects the head to the chest.

The man has a stiff neck.

nest

A home made by birds with twigs or moss to hold their eggs.

The nest has four eggs in it.

new

The opposite of old. Not been used before.

The bike is shiny and new.

newspaper

A set of large pages printed with stories and recent events.

The newspaper is full of Letterland news.

nice

Something that is pleasant or enjoyable.

It is nice to go to the beach.

a b c d e f g h i j k l m n o p q r s t u v w x y z

night

The time between evening and morning.

The stars come out at night.

nine

The word for the number 9.

Nine is Noisy Nick's favourite number.

noise

A sound you can hear.

Noisy Nick makes lots of noise.

noodles

Long strips of food made from flour, eggs and water.

Noodles are fun to eat.

north

The opposite of south.

Polar bears live at the North Pole.

nose

The part of the body on the face that you breathe and smell through.

Nick has two eyes, one nose and a mouth.

number

Symbols used in counting.

What number can you count up to?

nurse

Someone who looks after sick and injured people.

The nurse brought out the medicine.

nursery

A place for babies and young children to sleep, play and learn.

The boy is looked after well at the nursery.

a b c d e f g h i j k l m n o p q r s t u v w x y z

Oscar Orange says 'o...' at the start of his name. Here are some more words that start with his sound.

 = a decodable word

octopus
A sea animal with eight long legs.

The octopus lives in a cave at the bottom of the ocean.

ocean
Salt water that covers a lot of the earth.

The ocean is full of living things.

off
The opposite of on.

The light is switched off at night.

office
A place where people work.

The office is closed on Sundays.

old

Not young or new.

The man is very old.

on

The opposite of off.

Oscar is on the box.

open

The opposite of closed.

The door is open.

orange

A round, sweet fruit with an orange skin.

The orange is tasty and juicy.

otter

A brown animal that can swim well. It eats fish.

The otter is swimming.

Mr O

This is Mr O, the Old Man. He waves and says his name in words.

a b c d e f g h i j k l m n o p q r s t u v w x y z

Pp

Peter Puppy says 'p...' at the start of his name. Here are some more words that start with his sound.

 = a decodable word

paint

A liquid you put on things to add colour or to protect them.

There are paw prints in the paint.

paper

A material we can write and draw on or wrap things in.

The picture is painted on paper.

park

A place to go to enjoy, rest or have fun playing.

The children play at the park.

path

A narrow walk or cycle way.

The path leads to the park.

pear

A sweet, soft fruit with yellow, green or red skin.

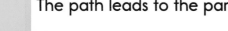

This pear looks ripe.

peas

Small, round, green seeds that we eat as a vegetable.

Mr E likes to eat peas.

pen

A long, thin object we use for writing or drawing in ink.

The pen has stopped working.

pencil

A long, thin object, often made from wood, used for writing or drawing.

This pencil has a sharp end.

phonics

A method of teaching reading by learning the speech sounds that letters make.

Let's learn phonics with Letterland!

photo

ph

A picture made using a camera.

The photo is of a ball.

plant

A living thing that usually grows in the earth and has leaves.

There is a new plant in the garden.

police

People who work to protect others and make sure everyone obeys laws.

The police were called to an emergency.

present

A gift or a prize usually wrapped up in paper.

The present is wrapped up for the party.

purse

A little bag used for carrying money or other small things.

The coins are kept in the purse.

The ph story

When Peter Puppy sits next to Harry Hat Man, Harry takes his photograph to make Peter happy.

a b c d e f g h i j k l m n o p q r s t u v w x y z

Quarrelsome Queen says 'q...' at the start of her name. Here are some more words that start with her sound.

☆ = a decodable word

quack

The noise a duck makes. (But not Dippy Duck!)

Ducks quack when they swim about.

quarry

A big pit from which stone or gravel has been dug.

The truck was full when it left the quarry.

quarter

One of four equal parts.

I am four and a quarter!

queen

A woman who rules a country, or the wife of a king.

This is Quarrelsome Queen.

question
A sentence that needs an answer.

The teacher asked a question.

queue
A line of people or things waiting for something.

There was a queue of trucks on the road.

quick
Moving with speed.

The boy has a quick run before school.

quiet
Not making much noise.

The boy is quiet while the dog sleeps.

quilt
A thick bed cover made with cloth stitched together.

The quilt has a lovely pattern.

quiz
Questions to test what someone knows.

The Queen writes the quiz questions.

R r

Red Robot says 'r...' at the start of his name. Here are some more words that start with his sound.

 = a decodable word

rabbit

A small animal with long ears that bounces along.

Red Robot likes rabbits.

race

A test of speed.

He won the race.

radio

A machine for listening to music or people talking.

The radio is very loud.

rain

Drops of water that fall from the clouds in the sky.

The rain is making the girl wet.

rainbow

A curved arc across the sky, with seven colours.

The rainbow is very beautiful.

rice

The seeds of a grass that grow in warm, wet places. We eat them.

The rice is in the bowl.

a b c d e f g h i j k l m n o p q r s t u v w x y z

right

Correct, or the opposite of left.

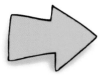

Our house is on the right side of the road.

ring

A small band of metal you can wear on your finger.

The ring sparkles in the light.

river

A large stream of water that goes to the sea or a lake.

The river flows through the valley.

road

A hard surface for cars and people to travel on.

The road is empty today.

robot

A machine that looks like a person that can do something for us.

The robot is a fun toy.

rocket

It goes up into the air quickly, powered by gases.

The rocket went up into space.

roof

The covering on top of a building.

Every house needs a roof to keep out the rain.

rope

Pieces of string twisted together to make a strong, thick line.

The boat was tied to the shore with a rope.

ruler

A straight piece of wood, metal or plastic you use for measuring things.

The boy measured 10cm with his ruler.

S s

a b c d e f g h i j k l m n o p q r **s** t u v w x y z

Sammy Snake says 's...' at the start of his name. Here are some more words that start with his sound.

 = a decodable word

sad
Not happy.

The little boy is sad.

sand
Tiny rocks you find on a beach and in some deserts.

Wet sand is perfect for building sandcastles.

sandwich
Slices of bread with food between them like meat, cheese or fish.

The sandwich has lettuce in it.

scarf
A long piece of material worn around the neck.

The scarf is stripy.

sea
Salt water that covers a lot of the earth.

The sea and the sky are blue.

sheep
A farm animal bred for meat and wool.

sh

The sheep is eating.

42

ship
sh

A form of transport that travels on water.

The ship sails on the sea.

shop
sh

A place where things are sold.

The shop is full of toys.

sky

The space high up above the earth.

There are clouds in the sky.

snow

Small soft pieces of frozen water that fall from the sky.

The snow covers the trees and houses.

soap

Something used for washing and cleaning.

The soap smells of flowers.

spoon

A tool for eating food, to stir or measure.

I eat my soup with a spoon.

star

Dots of light seen twinkling in the night sky.

One star is brighter than the others.

sun

The star that is closest to the earth.

The sun is warm.

The sh story

When Sammy Snake slithers up behind Harry Hat Man making lots of noise, Harry turns and says, 'sh!'

a b c d e f g h i j k l m n o p q r s t u v w x y z

43

Talking Tess says 't...' at the start of her name. Here are some more words that start with her sound.

⭐ = a decodable word

table

A piece of furniture with a flat surface and legs.

This table is made from wood.

teacher

Someone who helps others to learn.

The children like their teacher.

teddy

A child's soft toy that looks like a bear.

The teddy is soft and cuddly.

television

A machine showing moving pictures with sound.

Dad watches the news on the television.

ten

The word for the number 10.

Tess's favourite number is ten.

thank you

Words said or written to express thanks.

The boy wrote to say thank you to his grandma.

th

three
The word for the number 3.

Three is the number before four.

tiger
A large, strong cat with light fur and black stripes.

The tiger prowls through the jungle.

towel
A cloth used for drying things.

This towel belongs to Talking Tess.

town
A group of houses and buildings, smaller than a city.

The train travels across the bridge into the town.

toy
An object you can play with.

The toys are in the toy box.

tractor
A machine with big tyres, used for farm work.

The tractor is red.

train
A form of transport that travels on tracks.

The train is on time.

tree
A tall plant with a trunk, many branches and leaves.

The tree is green in summer.

The th story
When these two are together in words, there's thunder about. Tess comforts Harry, "There, there. It's only the thunder."

a b c d e f g h i j k l m n o p q r s **t** u v w x y z

umbrella
An object you put above your head to protect you from the rain.

The umbrella has a blue handle.

under
Below something.

The children are sheltering under the umbrella.

underwear
Clothing you wear next to your skin, under other clothes.

The underwear is on the washing line.

unicycle
A form of transport with one wheel.

It is very wobbly on the unicycle!

uniform

Special clothes worn by people in a group or school.

The uniform is very smart.

unwell

Feeling sick or ill.

The boy feels unwell.

up

Towards a higher place.

The arrow points up.

upset

Feeling sad or hurt.

The boy feels upset.

upside down

When the part usually at the top is at the bottom.

The umbrella is upside down.

Mr U

This is Mr U, the Uniform Man. He waves and says his name in words.

Vicky Violet says 'v...' at the start of her name. Here are some more words that start with her sound.

 = a decodable word

van

A form of transport used to carry people or objects.

Vicky Violet's vegetables are in her van.

vase

An open container you can put flowers in.

The vase is empty.

vegetables

Part of a plant that is used for food.

I like vegetables with my dinner.

vet

A doctor for animals.

The vet made the cat feel better.

view

What is seen from a particular point.

The view is of the village in the valley.

village

A group of houses and buildings, smaller than a town.

The village has a school and a shop.

violin

A musical instrument with four strings played using a bow.

The girl played her violin in a concert.

volcano

An opening in the earth where fiery, melted rock comes out.

There is smoke coming from the top of this volcano.

vowel

The letters a, e, i, o, u and sometimes y.

The word 'ant' starts with a vowel.

vulture

A large bird, often with a bald head and neck.

The vulture is hungry.

Ww

wall

The side of a building or something that divides a room.

The builders made a new wall.

watch

A small clock that can be worn on the wrist.

The boy checked the time on his watch.

water

A clear liquid. People, plants and animals need water to survive.

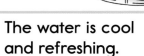

The water is cool and refreshing.

waves

Ridges that rise from the surface of the sea or a river.

The waves lap against the shore.

whale

A large mammal that lives in the sea.

The whale splashed and dived.

wheel

A round thing that turns to make some vehicles move.

The tractor's wheel is huge.

whistle

A small instrument that makes a high sound when it is blown.

The referee blows his whistle at the end of the game.

white

The colour of clean snow. The lightest colour.

The envelope is white.

wind

Air moving across the earth.

The wind blows the leaves.

window

A piece of glass in a building that lets in the light.

The window is open.

wood

The material that comes from a tree.

Some chairs are made from wood.

word

A group of sounds that mean something. Used when we speak and write.

The teacher spelled the word.

world

The earth and everything in it.

There is a map of the world on the wall.

worm

A small animal with a long, flexible body that lives in the soil.

The worm wiggled and wriggled.

The wh story

When Walter Walrus is behind Harry he can't see over the hat so he whooshes it off with a wave of water. Harry is too startled to speak.

Xx

Fix-it Max says 'x...' at the **end** of his name. Here are some more words that contain his sound.

 = a decodable word

axe
A tool used to cut down trees and chop wood.

The axe is sharp and heavy.

box
A container made of stiff material that usually has four sides, a bottom and a lid.

The box is open.

fox
A wild animal with a pointed nose and a bushy tail.

This fox can run fast.

saxophone
A musical instrument you blow into.

The children all want to play the saxophone.

six
The word for the number 6.

Fix-it Max is six years old.

X-ray
A photograph that shows the bones inside your body.

The doctor sent the boy for an X-ray.

a b c d e f g h i j k l m n o p q r s t u v w x y z

Yy

Yo-yo Man says 'y...' at the start of his name. Here are some more words that start with his sound.

⭐ = a decodable word

yawn
A deep breath taken with a wide open mouth, often when tired.

The teddy gives a huge yawn.

year
Twelve months or 365 days.

I hope the summer is hot this year.

yellow
The colour of the sun.

The sun looks like a yellow ball in the sky.

yogurt
A soft food make with sour milk.

The yogurt is kept in the fridge.

young
The early part of life.

The children are young.

yo-yo
A toy that goes up and down on a string.

The girl played with her yo-yo.

a b c d e f g h i j k l m n o p q r s t u v w x y z

Zig Zag Zebra says 'z...' at the start of her name. Here are some more words that start with her sound.

 = a decodable word

zebra
An animal that has black and white stripes.

The zebra lives in Africa.

zero
The word for the number 0.

0

Three, two, one, zero! The rocket launched.

zigzag
A line that turns from side to side sharply.

The girl drew a zigzag pattern in her sketchpad.

zip
Something you can pull to open and close bags or clothes.

The bag has a zip on it.

zoo
A place where animals are kept so people can look at them.

I like to visit the zoo.

a b c d e f g h i j k l m n o p q r s t u v w x y z

54

100 words we write a lot

1. the	26. are	51. do	76. about
2. and	27. up	52. me	77. got
3. a	28. had	53. down	78. their
4. to	29. my	54. dad	79. people
5. said	30. her	55. big	80. your
6. in	31. what	56. when	81. put
7. he	32. there	57. it's	82. could
8. I	33. out	58. see	83. house
9. of	34. this	59. looked	84. old
10. it	35. have	60. very	85. too
11. was	36. went	61. look	86. by
12. you	37. be	62. don't	87. day
13. they	38. like	63. come	88. made
14. on	39. some	64. will	89. time
15. she	40. so	65. into	90. I'm
16. is	41. not	66. back	91. if
17. for	42. then	67. from	92. help
18. at	43. were	68. children	93. Mrs
19. his	44. go	69. him	94. called
20. but	45. little	70. Mr	95. here
21. that	46. as	71. get	96. off
22. with	47. no	72. just	97. asked
23. all	48. mum	73. now	98. saw
24. we	49. one	74. came	99. make
25. can	50. them	75. oh	100. an

The alphabet

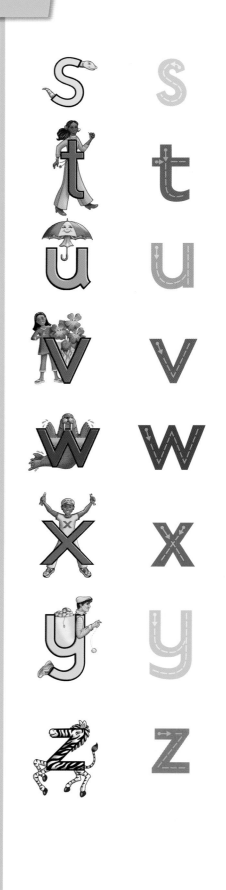

Days of the week

Monday   Tuesday   Wednesday   Thursday

Friday   Saturday   Sunday

Months of the year

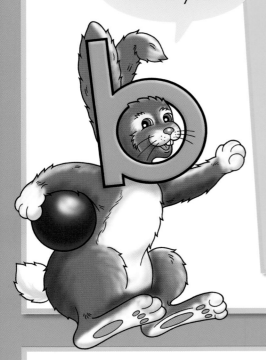

I love birthdays! When is yours?

- January -
- February -
- March -
- April -
- May -
- June -

- July -
- August -
- September -
- October -
- November -
- December -

Seasons

spring   summer   autumn   winter

Shapes

circle

triangle

square

diamond

star

oval

rectangle

hexagon

pentagon

Colours

red

yellow

blue

green

pink

purple

brown

black

1 one

6 six

2 two

7 seven

3 three

8 eight

4 four

9 nine

5 five

10 ten

Verbs

Verbs are 'doing' words. A verb usually expresses an action.

add	cry	grow
borrow	cut	hear 
bounce	dance	help
buy 	dig 	hop
call	drink 	jump
carry	drop	keep
catch 	eat	kick
clap	exercise	laugh 
climb	fall 	like
close	find 	listen
cook	fly	look

make		sit		use	
open		sleep		walk	
paint		smell		wash	
pay		smile		wave	
play		stop		win	
pull		take		write	
push		talk		yawn	
read		taste		yell	
run		think		
see		throw		
sing		touch		

Fun and games!

Word detective!

Use your dictionary to help Detective Dippy Duck discover which words are being described below.

- It is a musical instrument. It has strings. Golden Girl might play one. What is it?

- It is an animal with four legs and big ears. It has a trunk. What is it?

- It is a form of transport. It has one wheel. What is it?

Alphabet order

Can you put these things in alphabetical order?

Odd one out

Use your dictionary to help you work out the odd one out in the groups below.

jet ship helicopter

tiger hippo lion

banana grapes peas

The Letterlanders

Annie Apple   Bouncy Ben   Clever Cat   Dippy Duck   Eddy Elephant   Firefighter Fred

Golden Girl   Harry Hat Man   Impy Ink   Jumping Jim   Kicking King

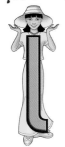    

Lucy Lamp Light   Munching Mike   Noisy Nick   Oscar Orange   Peter Puppy

Quarrelsome Queen   Red Robot   Sammy Snake   Talking Tess   Uppy Umbrella

Vicky Violet   Walter Walrus   Fix-it Max   Yellow Yo-yo Man   Zig Zag Zebra

Letterland®

Child-friendly phonics

The Letterland system teaches all 44 sounds in the English language through stories rather than rules. There are resources to take children from the very first stages of learning to full literacy.

ABC Trilogy

Handwriting Practice

My First & My Second Activity Books

Sticker & Activity Books

Picture Books

Games & Puzzles